W9-BML-406

# INTEGRATING
# American History
## with Reading Instruction

**6 Complete Social Studies Units**

### Written by
Trisha Callella

**Editor:** LaDawn Walter
**Illustrator:** Jenny Campbell
**Cover Illustrator:** Rick Grayson
**Designer/Production:** Moonhee Pak/Carrie Carter
**Cover Designer:** Moonhee Pak
**Art Director:** Tom Cochrane
**Project Director:** Carolea Williams

# Table of Contents

Introduction     3

Connections
to Standards     4

Unit Overview     5

## Early Explorers
Prereading Strategies . . . . . . . . . . 9
Nonfiction Text . . . . . . . . . . . . . . 12
Postreading Applications . . . . . 14
Hands-on Social Studies . . . . . . . 17

## Colonization
Prereading Strategies . . . . . . . . . 19
Nonfiction Text . . . . . . . . . . . . . . 22
Postreading Applications . . . . . 24
Hands-on Social Studies . . . . . . . 27

## Women of the American Revolution
Prereading Strategies . . . . . . . . . 30
Nonfiction Text . . . . . . . . . . . . . . 33
Postreading Applications . . . . . 35
Hands-on Social Studies . . . . . . . 38

## Slavery
Prereading Strategies . . . . . . . . . 42
Nonfiction Text . . . . . . . . . . . . . . 45
Postreading Applications . . . . . 47
Hands-on Social Studies . . . . . . 50

## Industrial Revolution
Prereading Strategies . . . . . . . . . 53
Nonfiction Text . . . . . . . . . . . . . . 56
Postreading Applications . . . . . 58
Hands-on Social Studies . . . . . . . 61

## Civil War
Prereading Strategies . . . . . . . . . 63
Nonfiction Text . . . . . . . . . . . . . . 66
Postreading Applications . . . . . 68
Hands-on Social Studies . . . . . . . 71

# Introduction

For many students, reading comprehension diminishes when they read nonfiction text. Students often have difficulty understanding social studies vocabulary, making inferences, and grasping social studies concepts. With so much curriculum to cover each day, social studies content is sometimes put on the back burner when it comes to academic priorities. *Integrating American History with Reading Instruction* provides the perfect integration of social studies content with specific reading instruction to help students improve their comprehension of nonfiction text and maximize every minute of your teaching day.

This resource includes six units that relate to American history. The units are based on the most common social studies topics taught in fifth grade in accordance with the national social studies standards:

**Early Explorers**            **Slavery**
**Colonization**               **Industrial Revolution**
**Women of the American Revolution**  **Civil War**

Each unit includes powerful prereading strategies, such as predicting what the story will be about, accessing prior knowledge, and brainstorming about vocabulary that may be included in the reading selection. Following the prereading exercises is a nonfiction reading selection written on a fifth grade reading level. Each reading selection is followed by essential postreading activities such as comprehension questions on multiple taxonomy levels, skill reviews, and a critical thinking exercise. Each unit also includes a hands-on activity that connects each social studies topic to students' lives. The descriptions on pages 5–8 include the objectives and implementation strategies for each unit component.

Before, during, and after reading the story, students are exposed to the same reading strategies you typically reinforce during your language arts instruction block and guided reading. This powerful duo gives you the opportunity to teach both reading and social studies simultaneously. Using the activities in this resource, children will continue *learning to read* while *reading to learn*. They will become more successful readers while gaining new social studies knowledge and experiences.

**Prereading Strategies**

✓ Catch a Clue
✓ Concept Map
✓ Word Warm-Up

**Nonfiction Text**

**Postreading Applications**

✓ Comprehension Questions
✓ Sharpen Your Skills
✓ Get Logical

**Hands-on Social Studies**

# Connections to Standards

This chart shows the concepts that are covered in each unit based on the national social studies standards.

| | Early Explorers | Colonization | Women of the American Revolution | Slavery | Industrial Revolution | Civil War |
|---|:---:|:---:|:---:|:---:|:---:|:---:|
| Compare and contrast differences about past events, people, places, or situations, and identify how they contribute to our understanding of the past. | ● | ● | ● | ● | ● | ● |
| Identify and describe selected historical periods and patterns of change within and across cultures. | ● | ● | ● | ● | ● | ● |
| Recognize examples of cause and effect relationships. | ● | ● | ● | ● | ● | ● |
| Develop critical sensitivities such as empathy and skepticism regarding attitudes, values, and behaviors of people in different historical contexts. | ● | ● | ● | ● | ● | ● |
| Relate personal changes to social, cultural, and historical contexts. | ● | ● | ● | ● | ● | ● |
| Describe personal connections to places such as community, nation, and world. | ● | ● | ● | ● | ● | ● |
| Work independently and cooperatively to accomplish goals. | ● | ● | ● | ● | ● | ● |
| Identify and analyze examples of tensions between expressions of individuality and group efforts to promote social conformity. | | ● | | ● | | ● |
| Explain conditions, actions, and motivations that contribute to conflict and cooperation within and among nations. | ● | ● | ● | ● | ● | ● |
| Describe examples in which values, beliefs, and attitudes have been influenced by new scientific and technological knowledge. | | | | | ● | |
| Give examples of conflict, cooperation, and interdependence among individuals, groups, and nations. | | ● | ● | ● | ● | ● |
| Investigate concerns, issues, standards, and conflicts related to universal human rights such as religious groups and the effects of war. | | ● | ● | ● | ● | ● |

# Unit Overview

## Catch a Clue

### Objectives

Students will

✓ be introduced to key concepts and vocabulary *before* reading

✓ be able to transfer this key strategy to improve test-taking skills

### Implementation

Students will use clues and the process of elimination to predict what the nonfiction reading selection will be about. Copy this page on an overhead transparency, and use it for a whole-class activity. Begin by reading aloud each word, and ask students to repeat the words. Read the clues one at a time. Then, discuss with the class what topic(s) could be eliminated and the reasons why. (Note: There will be clues that do not eliminate any topics. The purpose of this is to teach students that although there is information listed, it is not always helpful information.) Cross off a topic when the class decides that it does not fit the clues. If there is more than one topic left after the class discusses all of the clues, this becomes a prediction activity. When this occurs, reread the clues with the class, and discuss which answer would be most appropriate given the clues provided.

## Concept Map

### Objectives

Students will

✓ access prior knowledge by brainstorming what they already know about the topic

✓ increase familiarity with the social studies content by hearing others' prior knowledge experiences

✓ revisit the map *after* reading to recall information from the reading selection

### Implementation

Copy this page on an overhead transparency, and use it for a whole-class activity. Use a colored pen to write students' prior knowledge on the transparency. After the class reads the story, use a different colored pen to add what students learned.

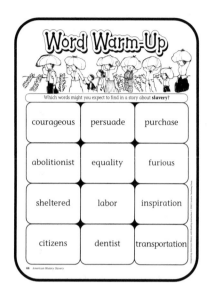

# Word Warm-Up

## Objectives

Students will

✓ be introduced to new vocabulary words

✓ make predictions about the story using thinking and reasoning skills

✓ begin to monitor their own comprehension

## Implementation

Students will use the strategy of exclusion brainstorming to identify which words are likely to be in the story and which words are unrelated and should be eliminated from the list. Copy this page on an overhead transparency, and use it for a whole-class activity. Have students make predictions about which of the vocabulary words could be in the story and which words probably would not be in the story. Ask them to give reasons for their predictions. For example, say *Do you think a dentist would be in a story about slavery?* A student may say *Yes, because a dentist could have owned a slave* or *No, because a dentist relates to a person's career, not slavery.* Circle the word if a student says that it will be in the story, and cross it out if a student says it will not be in the story. Do not correct students' responses. After reading, students can either confirm or disconfirm their own predictions. It is more powerful for students to verify their predictions on their own than to be told the answer before ever reading the story.

## Nonfiction Text

# The Story

## Objectives

Students will

✓ read high-interest, nonfiction stories

✓ increase social studies knowledge

✓ increase content area vocabulary

✓ make connections between social studies facts and their own experiences

## Implementation

Give each student a copy of the story, and display the corresponding Word Warm-Up transparency while you read the story with the class. After the class reads the story, go back to the transparency, and have students discuss their predictions in relation to the new information they learned in the story. Invite students to identify any changes they would make on the transparency and give reasons for their responses. Then, revisit the corresponding Concept Map transparency, and write the new information students have learned.

# Postreading Applications

## Comprehension Questions

### Objectives

Students will

✓ recall factual information

✓ be challenged to think beyond the story facts to make inferences

✓ connect the story to other reading, their own lives, and the world around them

### Implementation

Use these questions to facilitate a class discussion of the story. Choose the number and types of questions that best meet the abilities of your class.

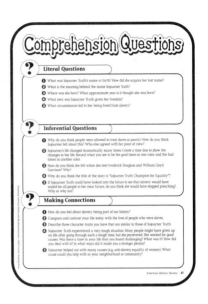

## Sharpen Your Skills

### Objectives

Students will

✓ practice answering questions in common test-taking formats

✓ integrate language arts skills with social studies knowledge

### Implementation

After the class reads a story, give each student a copy of this page. Ask students to read each question and all of the answer choices for that question before deciding on an answer. Show them how to use their pencil to completely fill in the circle for their answer. Invite students to raise their hand if they have difficulty reading a question and/or the answer choices. Thoroughly explain the types of questions and exactly what is being asked the first few times students use this reproducible.

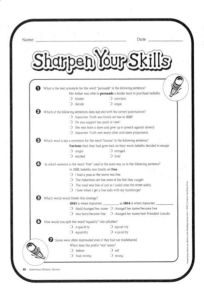

# Get Logical

## Objectives

Students will

✓ practice logical and strategic thinking skills

✓ practice the skill of process of elimination

✓ transfer the information read by applying it to new situations

## Implementation

Give each student a copy of this page. Read the beginning sentences and the clues to familiarize students with the words. Show students step-by-step how to eliminate choices based on the clues given. Have students place an X in a box that represents an impossible choice, thereby narrowing down the options for accurate choices. Once students understand the concept, they can work independently on this reproducible.

# Hands-on Social Studies

# Social Studies Activity

## Objectives

Students will

✓ participate in hands-on learning experiences

✓ expand and reinforce social studies knowledge

✓ apply new social studies vocabulary words

## Implementation

The social studies activities in this book incorporate a variety of skills students are required to experience at this age level (e.g., survey, interview, analyze, evaluate). Each hands-on activity begins with an explanation of its purpose to help direct the intended learning. Give each student a copy of any corresponding reproducibles and/or materials for the activity. Then, introduce the activity and explain the directions. Model any directions that may be difficult for students to follow on their own.

# Catch a Clue

**What will we learn about in our reading today?**

how the United States were formed

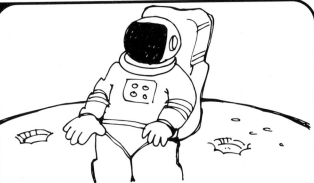

the first person to walk on the moon

who signed the Declaration of Independence

early explorers of America

**1** We will not learn about any of the New England states.

**2** We will learn about a group of people who did something "first."

**3** We will learn about some individuals who traveled to new lands in search of new resources.

**4** We will learn about some voyages in the late 1400s and early 1500s.

# Concept Map

Facts we already know about **early explorers,** and the new facts we have learned

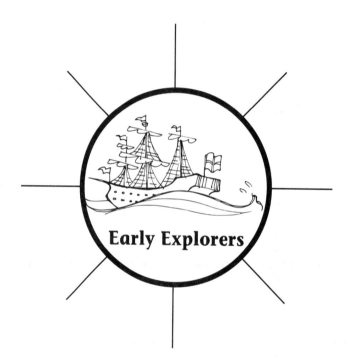

**Early Explorers**

*Integrating American History with Reading Instruction © 2002 Creative Teaching Press*

# Word Warm-Up

Which words might you expect to find in a story about **early explorers?**

| | | |
|---|---|---|
| voyage | pirates | Asia |
| Italy | king | navigator |
| transport | business | merchant |
| geographer | expensive | expedition |

# What's in a Name?

Christopher Columbus is often credited with the discovery of America. So why isn't our country called the United States of Columbus? Why don't we live on the continent of North Columbus? Why do we live in a country named America?

On his first voyage, Columbus landed in what would become known as North America. Actually, he landed on the islands of the Caribbean. He was searching for another route to Asia and India. He thought he was in India. He thought his voyage was a success.

Columbus later explored the coast of South America, too. He still thought he was on his way to India. He had no idea that he was on a new continent. Even the people back home in Europe thought Columbus had landed on the Asian continent.

Amerigo Vespucci thought differently. Vespucci was a navigator who was the first to identify North and South America as new continents. He believed that these new continents were not at all connected to Asia.

Amerigo Vespucci was born in Florence, Italy in 1454. He read and studied. He collected books and maps. He became a navigator and a merchant. He first went to work for the Medici family, a rich and powerful family in Italy. Then, in 1492, he moved to Seville, Spain. In 1495, he took over the business of a merchant in Seville. The business sold supplies to ships that were on their way to explore the West Indies. Later, Vespucci decided to make a voyage himself.

Vespucci claimed that he voyaged to South America in 1497. This would have made him the first European on the mainland of America. However, some people who study history do not think this is true. They think he made his first voyage in 1499. On that voyage, Vespucci sailed with a Spanish expedition to South America. He made other voyages with Portuguese expeditions in 1501 and 1503. Some people do not believe that he ever led an expedition himself.

*Integrating American History with Reading Instruction © 2002 Creative Teaching Press*

Amerigo Vespucci kept detailed records and maps of his explorations in the New World. Vespucci combined his accounts with those of other explorers. He studied all the information he had. He decided that this new land was not part of Asia or of any known continent. Vespucci decided that the new land was a new continent.

The maps and records of Amerigo Vespucci were translated and sold as a book in Europe. People enjoyed reading about his voyages and discoveries. People thought his accounts were much more interesting than those recorded by Christopher Columbus.

Martin Waldseemüller was a mapmaker and geographer living in Germany. He had the job of translating Vespucci's records. As he read Vespucci's accounts, he agreed that the New World was indeed a new continent. Waldseemüller loved to make up names when he created his maps. So he used Vespucci's given name, Amerigo, and changed it a little. He thought the name "America" was a proper one for this new land. In 1507, the name America was used for the first time.

It did not take long for two more explorers to prove that Amerigo Vespucci was right. Vasco Núñez de Balboa explored the area of Panama for Spain. He crossed the strait of Panama and viewed the ocean on the other side. He was the first European to see the Pacific Ocean. Balboa realized this huge body of water must separate the Americas from Asia. Then, a Portuguese navigator, Ferdinand Magellan, tried to sail around the world. In 1520, he sailed around Cape Horn at the tip of South America. When his ship reached the next ocean, it seemed so calm and peaceful he named it the Pacific Ocean.

So America was named for a nearly unknown merchant and seaman from Italy. This thought must have occurred to Waldseemüller as well because he later tried to change the name. He could not. The name America seemed to have stuck in people's minds. In 1538, the names "North America" and "South America" were used for the first time on a map of the world.

# Comprehension Questions

## Literal Questions

❶ Who was Amerigo Vespucci? Where was he from? What is he known for?

❷ Who was Ferdinand Magellan? What is he known for?

❸ Who was Martin Waldseemüller? Where did he live? What did he do?

❹ What important dates relate to the discovery of America? Make a time line, and explain what each date represents.

❺ How was America given its name? When was the name "America" used for the first time?

## Inferential Questions

❶ Who really first discovered America? Why do people say it was Christopher Columbus?

❷ Why is the nation called the United States of America?

❸ Why do you think Amerigo Vespucci is not any more famous than he is?

❹ Compare and contrast Christopher Columbus and Amerigo Vespucci. List at least two ways that they are similar and two ways each early explorer is unique.

❺ If Christopher Columbus and Amerigo Vespucci met each other, what do you think each would say to the other? Write down a short conversation between the two men.

## Making Connections

❶ If you could discover a new island and have it named after yourself, what would it be called? Why?

❷ You know the rhyme "In 1492 Columbus sailed the ocean blue." Make up a rhyme for the name Amerigo Vespucci to remind others who America was named after and the year America was named.

❸ List some character traits you think these early explorers must have had. Describe three character traits you have that are similar to those of the early explorers.

❹ If you could be one of these early explorers, which person would you be? Why? What things would you do the same, and what things would you do differently?

❺ If you could travel back in time to ask any of these early explorers one question, which person would you choose? Why? What would you ask that person?

*Integrating American History with Reading Instruction © 2002 Creative Teaching Press*

# Sharpen Your Skills

**1** Which word is a synonym for "detailed" in the following sentence?

Amerigo Vespucci kept **detailed** records and maps of his explorations in the New World.

- ○ missing
- ○ expensive
- ○ thorough
- ○ sloppy

**2** If you wanted to learn more about Amerigo Vespucci, which resource would be the most helpful?

- ○ dictionary
- ○ encyclopedia
- ○ atlas
- ○ thesaurus

**3** What part of speech is the word "and" in the following sentence?

You wrote a good report **and** gave a terrific speech on Vespucci!

- ○ verb
- ○ adverb
- ○ adjective
- ○ conjunction

**4** In which sentence is the word "back" used in the same way as in the following sentence?

Even the people **back** home in Europe thought Columbus had landed on the Asian continent.

- ○ Did you hurt your back?
- ○ Give that book back to me.
- ○ His friends back at his old school were studying Magellan.
- ○ She gave him a ride on her back.

**5** Which words would finish this analogy?

**Waldseemüller** is to _____ as **Vespucci** is to _____.

- ○ South Africa/Italy
- ○ Germany/Italy
- ○ Italy/Germany
- ○ Germany/South Africa

**6** What are the words "sea" and "see" in the following sentence?

Early explorers sailed the **sea** to **see** if they could reach a new land.

- ○ synonyms
- ○ antonyms
- ○ homophones
- ○ heteronyms

**7** How would you split the word "America" into syllables?

- ○ A-meri-ca
- ○ A-mer-i-ca
- ○ Am-er-ica
- ○ Amer-i-ca

The index for a book on early explorers shows five chapters. Use the clues below to identify the title of each chapter.

## Clues

❶ "Christopher Columbus" was not the title of an even-numbered chapter, nor was it the last chapter.

❷ Ferdinand Magellan and Vasco Núñez de Balboa were not in the first chapter.

❸ Each explorer was written about in a separate chapter before the chapter titled "Hardships and Obstacles."

❹ The person who America was named after was mentioned in chapter 2.

❺ The man who crossed the strait of Panama and viewed the ocean on the other side was in a chapter before the chapter that discussed the Portuguese navigator who tried to sail around the world.

| | Chapter 1 | Chapter 2 | Chapter 3 | Chapter 4 | Chapter 5 |
|---|---|---|---|---|---|
| Ferdinand Magellan | | | | | |
| Amerigo Vespucci | | | | | |
| Christopher Columbus | | | | | |
| Vasco Núñez de Balboa | | | | | |
| Hardships and Obstacles | | | | | |

Chapter 1 was titled _____.

Chapter 2 was titled _____.

Chapter 3 was titled _____.

Chapter 4 was titled _____.

Chapter 5 was titled _____.

*Integrating American History with Reading Instruction © 2002 Creative Teaching Press*

# Exploration: A Puzzling Process

## Purpose

The purpose of this activity is for students to reinforce the information they learned about early explorers of America.

Integrating American History with Reading Instruction © 2002 Creative Teaching Press

### MATERIALS

✔ Early Explorers Crossword Puzzle (page 18)
✔ overhead transparency/ projector (optional)
✔ graph paper (optional)
✔ lined paper (optional)

## Implementation

Give each student an Early Explorers Crossword Puzzle. Have students read each clue and write the correct answer in the corresponding answer space. If this is a new format for students, make an overhead transparency of the reproducible, and complete the first few questions together as a whole group. As an extension, give each student a piece of graph paper and lined paper. Invite students to write their own questions and answers on the lined paper and create a crossword puzzle on the graph paper. Encourage students to exchange their questions and crossword puzzle with a partner and complete each other's puzzle.

**Answer Key**

Across
1. Vespucci
3. Magellan
5. Medici
6. Amerigo
8. India
9. Balboa

Down
2. Waldseemüller
4. Spain
7. Caribbean
10. Europe

# Early Explorers Crossword Puzzle

**Directions:** Read each clue. Write your answer in the corresponding answer boxes using all capital letters.

## Across

1. He claimed that he voyaged to South America in 1497.
3. He tried to sail around the world. In 1520, he sailed around Cape Horn at the tip of South America. He later gave the Pacific Ocean its name.
5. The name of the rich and powerful family that Amerigo Vespucci first went to work for.
6. America was named after Vespucci's first name. What was it?
8. Columbus first thought he had sailed to this country during his first voyage.
9. He was the first European to see the Pacific Ocean.

## Down

2. He was a mapmaker and geographer living in Germany.
4. The country for which Vasco Núñez de Balboa explored the area of Panama.
7. Where did Columbus's first voyage lead him?
10. These early explorers were from which continent?

*Integrating American History with Reading Instruction © 2002 Creative Teaching Press*

# Catch a Clue

## What will we learn about in our reading today?

colonization

Native Americans

the Pony Express

the Gold Rush

**1** People working together as a group is an important part of this topic.

**2** We will learn about situations of the past that no longer exist today.

**3** We will not be learning about events that took place in California.

**4** We will learn how the export of tobacco assisted in the survival of an area.

# Concept Map

Facts we already know about **colonization,** and the new facts we have learned

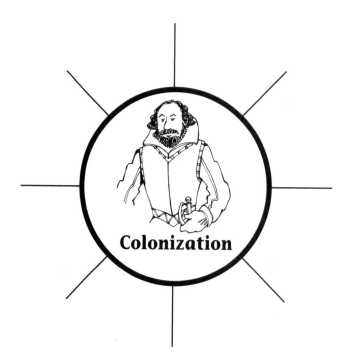

**Colonization**

*Integrating American History with Reading Instruction © 2002 Creative Teaching Press*

# Word Warm-Up

Which words might you expect to find in a story about **colonization?**

| | | |
|---|---|---|
| adventurers | biography | debtors |
| survival | settlement | alcohol |
| plantations | tobacco | governed |
| equality | reformers | royal |

Integrating American History with Reading Instruction © 2002 Creative Teaching Press

# What Makes a Colony?

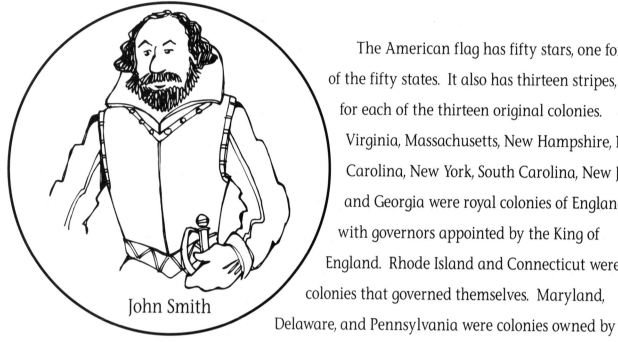

John Smith

The American flag has fifty stars, one for each of the fifty states. It also has thirteen stripes, one for each of the thirteen original colonies. Virginia, Massachusetts, New Hampshire, North Carolina, New York, South Carolina, New Jersey, and Georgia were royal colonies of England with governors appointed by the King of England. Rhode Island and Connecticut were colonies that governed themselves. Maryland, Delaware, and Pennsylvania were colonies owned by individual people.

What is a colony? A colony is a place that belongs to another country. It is a land controlled by a foreign nation. The people who come to live in the colony intend to live there permanently. However, these people keep the citizenship of the foreign country. The first colonies in North America were founded for a number of reasons. Companies started some colonies to make money. Other colonies were founded by reformers who dreamed of a perfect society. Religious groups wanting to practice their beliefs in peace started other colonies.

Jamestown was an English settlement in North America founded by the Virginia Company of London in 1607. This company got permission from King James I of England to start a settlement for the purpose of making a profit from the New World. The first citizens of Jamestown were gentleman adventurers. They expected to get rich fast and did not expect to have to work for it. They could not have picked a worse place for a colony, either. Within three months, starvation and illness had left only a few of the original group alive.

Captain John Smith was a strong leader who did survive. He realized that if Jamestown were to succeed, he would need better workers. He asked the Virginia Company to send him men who would work hard and had skills useful for the colony. The Virginia Company also promised to give

*Integrating American History with Reading Instruction © 2002 Creative Teaching Press*

land to people who went to Jamestown. This promise brought many farmers to Jamestown. They were needed to raise the food necessary for the colony's survival.

Jamestown almost failed on a number of occasions. In the end, it survived because of several events. When the Virginia Company of London went bankrupt, the King of England made Virginia a royal colony. It also helped that women had come to join the men in Jamestown. This meant that families would help its population to grow. Most importantly, Jamestown found a real moneymaker: tobacco. The export of tobacco from Virginia made the survival of this colony valuable to England.

The colony of Georgia was established for a different reason. Founded in 1732, King George II gave James Oglethorpe permission to start the colony of Georgia. He named Georgia in the king's honor. Oglethorpe planned Georgia to solve a problem. In England, if a person could not pay his debts, he could be thrown into debtor's prison. He would remain there until the debts were paid. However, he could not make money while in prison. It was a problem for the debtors.

Oglethorpe wanted to give debtors a chance to come to his colony of Georgia instead of going to jail. He wanted to make Georgia the ideal place to live. He banned alcohol and slavery in his colony. He wanted the colony to be made up of small farms and not big plantations. This way many people could become landowners and be responsible for raising their own food. Georgia attracted people from England with a variety of backgrounds and religions.

The colony was not the success that Oglethorpe wanted. The new colonists did not agree with his idea of a perfect society. They wanted to drink alcohol. They wanted to own slaves. They really wanted to have big plantations. In the end, James Oglethorpe went broke and gave up Georgia. In 1752, Georgia became another royal colony of England.

The story of each colony is different. Yet, it was the problems these colonies faced and the solutions they found that helped them survive. These qualities became the seeds for democratic ideas and one day the colonies would join together to form a new nation.

# Comprehension Questions

## Literal Questions

❶ What is a colony?

❷ What was the first permanent English settlement? Where was it located? Why was it started?

❸ Name three different reasons why colonies were started.

❹ What happened to Georgia in 1752? Why?

❺ What were some of the problems some of the original colonies faced?

## Inferential Questions

❶ Which reason to start a colony would convince you to be a colonist? Why?

❷ What impact did England have on the beginning of America?

❸ What symbol do we have in remembrance of the original thirteen colonies? Why were the original colonies important?

❹ Why do you think Oglethorpe wanted to ban alcohol and slavery in his colony?

❺ Think about James Oglethorpe's reasons for starting the colony of Georgia. Do you think they were good reasons? Why or why not? Can you think of anything he could have done that might have helped his plan?

## Making Connections

❶ If you were an early colonist, which type of colony (e.g., royal colony, self-governing colony, colony owned by individuals) would you want to live in? Why?

❷ In your opinion, was colonization a good idea? Why or why not?

❸ Name three problems you would have faced as a colonist. What would you have done to fix these problems? Name three benefits of being an early colonist.

❹ James Oglethorpe wanted to create a perfect society. If you could create a perfect society, what would it include?

❺ Compare and contrast Jamestown with the colony of Georgia.

*Integrating American History with Reading Instruction © 2002 Creative Teaching Press*

# Sharpen Your Skills

**1** Look at these words—debtor, actor, and translator.

What does the suffix "or" indicate?
- ○ the process of
- ○ a person who
- ○ without
- ○ the study of

**2** Which word best completes the following sentence?

Oglethorpe wanted to give debtors a chance to _____ in his colony of Georgia instead of going to jail.
- ○ came
- ○ work
- ○ gone
- ○ went

**3** What does the word "succeed" mean in the following sentence?

He realized that if Jamestown were to **succeed,** he would need better workers.
- ○ be successful
- ○ conquer
- ○ fail
- ○ persuade

**4** What is the best antonym for the word "ideal" in this sentence?

Oglethorpe wanted to make Georgia the **ideal** place to live.
- ○ worst
- ○ best
- ○ perfect
- ○ most wonderful

**5** Which words would finish this analogy?

**James Oglethorpe** is to _____ as **John Smith** is to _____.
- ○ Virginia/Maryland
- ○ Maryland/Massachusetts
- ○ Maryland/Virginia
- ○ Georgia/Virginia

**6** What kind of sentence is the following sentence?

The first citizens of Jamestown expected to get rich fast and did not expect to have to work for it but they could not have picked a worse place for a colony, since starvation and illness had left only a few of the original group alive.
- ○ simple sentence
- ○ complex sentence
- ○ fragment
- ○ run-on

**7** Which word best completes the following sentence?

The colonists did not _____ that starvation was going to be such a problem.
- ○ knew
- ○ known
- ○ no
- ○ know

Integrating American History with Reading Instruction © 2002 Creative Teaching Press

# Get Logical

Pauli, Megan, Pedro, Chi, and Maria are making a documentary about the early colonies with Pauli's new video camera. Each friend had a different speaking part. Read the dialogues below to decide who discussed each topic related to colonization in early America.

## Clues

❶ One of Megan's segments included her saying, "As you can see, starvation was a key problem for the colonists."

❷ The comment, "In 1607, it was founded by the Virginia Company of London," was not made by Maria, Chi, or Pauli.

❸ Pauli said, "James Oglethorpe went broke and gave it up. In 1752, it became another royal colony of England."

❹ The segment that included someone saying, "I need the Virginia Company to send me men who are used to working and have skills useful for the colony," was not narrated by Pedro or Maria.

|  | Pauli | Megan | Pedro | Chi | Maria |
|---|---|---|---|---|---|
| Jamestown |  |  |  |  |  |
| Georgia |  |  |  |  |  |
| John Smith |  |  |  |  |  |
| Hardships |  |  |  |  |  |
| Government |  |  |  |  |  |

Pauli narrated the segment on _____.

Megan narrated the segment on _____.

Pedro narrated the segment on _____.

Chi narrated the segment on _____.

Maria narrated the segment on _____.

*Integrating American History with Reading Instruction* © 2002 Creative Teaching Press

# Classroom Colonization

## Purpose

The purpose of this activity is for students to gain a deeper understanding of the original colonies and how they were created. Students will also practice using research materials, writing and presenting a report, and creating and constructing a mock colony.

### MATERIALS

- ✔ Colony Research reproducible (page 28)
- ✔ Classroom Colony reproducible (page 29)
- ✔ research materials (e.g., Internet, historical fiction books, encyclopedias)
- ✔ blank paper
- ✔ art supplies (e.g., craft sticks, sugar cubes, clay)

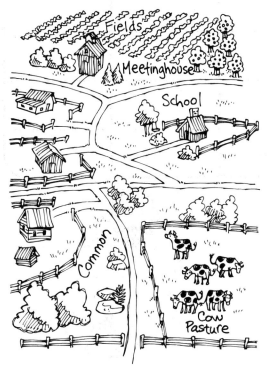

## Implementation

### Part 1

Give each student a Colony Research reproducible. Divide the class into groups of four students. Brainstorm with the class several historical colony groups (e.g., Roanoake, Jamestown, Plymouth Rock, St. Augustine), and write the name of each colony on the chalkboard. Invite each group to pick one colony to research. Provide a variety of research materials for students to use. Have each group member research one of the four subject areas listed on the reproducible. Tell students they will write a section about their subject for their group's report, present this information to the class, and create an appropriate visual aid. Invite groups to present their completed report to the class.

### Part 2

Tell students they have just gone back in time hundreds of years and no longer have the rules, government, food, and shelter of their current life. Tell them they will need to create their own colony from scratch! Give each group a Classroom Colony reproducible. Review the reproducible with the class. Ask students to think about and discuss the creation of their colony and write each answer in the space provided. Have groups draw on a piece of blank paper a map of their colony's location, keeping in mind the geography of the land and what they would need to be successful (e.g., water, tillable land, game). Ask groups to use art supplies such as craft sticks, sugar cubes, and clay to build a model of their colony. Tell students to consider aspects such as protection, space for crops, housing, community property, and historical authenticity. Invite groups to share their new colony, model, and map with the class.

# Colony Research

**Group Member Names:** _____

_____

**Directions:** Use research materials such as the Internet, encyclopedias, and historical fiction books to gather information about your colony. Use the outline below as a guide for finding information. Divide the sections below so that each member of your group has a section to research.

**Colony to Research:** _____

### I. Geography
    A.   Location
    B.   Climate
    C.   Natural Resources

### II. Leadership
    A.   Leadership of the Colony
    B.   Expectations and Rules for the People in the Colony
    C.   How Rules Were Enforced
    D.   Problems Encountered within the Colony

### III. Colony History
    A.   Why It Was Formed
    B.   Financial Backing
    C.   What They Hoped to Achieve

### IV. Other Interesting Facts
    A.   Jobs
    B.   Shelter
    C.   Food
    D.   Religion/Church
    E.   Education

**Presentation:** Combine the information from each section above into one well-written, final draft research report that includes a title page, table of contents, and bibliography. Assign one of the four sections listed above to each member of your group as a speaking part. Then, have each person create a visual aid (e.g., a location map, diagram of the colony, portrait of individuals) to accompany his or her speaking part. Be prepared to give a 10-minute group presentation on your colony to the class.

*Integrating American History with Reading Instruction © 2002 Creative Teaching Press*

# Classroom Colony

**Members of Our Colony:** _____

_____

**Directions:** Think about and discuss each question below with your group. When your group has agreed on an answer, write it in the space provided.

**1** The name of our colony is _____ because

_____

**2** What will the rules for your colony be?

_____

**3** How will these rules be enforced?

_____

**4** What jobs will be needed to run your colony?

_____

**5** How will you get food?

_____

**6** How will you have shelter?

_____

**7** Will your colony have a religion and/or a church? _____ What will it be?
_____ How will you build a church? _____

_____

**8** Will there be a school in your colony? _____ What will be included in your school?

_____

**9** Who will be the leader of your colony? _____ Why? _____

_____

**10** How will you protect your colony?

_____

Integrating American History with Reading Instruction © 2002 Creative Teaching Press

# Catch a Clue

women in the
Civil War

women who
were slaves

women in the
American
Revolution

women in the
abolitionist
movement

**1** We will learn about women who volunteered during a time of war.

**2** We will not discuss women who directly fought for women to have the right to vote, own land, and go to college.

**3** The women we will learn about were not involved in a war where the North fought against the South.

**4** We will meet the female Paul Revere!

*Integrating American History with Reading Instruction © 2002 Creative Teaching Press*

# Concept Map

Facts we already know about **women of the American Revolution,** and the new facts we have learned

**Women of the American Revolution**

# Word Warm-Up

Which words might you expect to find in a story about **women of the American Revolution?**

| | | |
|---|---|---|
| ribbons | militia | wagons |
| industry | explosion | resistance |
| regiment | obstacles | captured |
| responsibility | colonel | independence |

*Integrating American History with Reading Instruction © 2002 Creative Teaching Press*

# Women of the American Revolution

The American Revolution was the war fought between the thirteen colonies in America and Great Britain. This war was fought by the colonies to gain independence from the British. American men were called to serve in the Continental Army. American women did their part by staying home to care for the farms, businesses, and their families. Women were also asked to boycott tea, cloth, ribbons, and other British goods. However, some women chose to get right into the middle of the action.

Martha Bratton was one such woman. She lived in South Carolina. In her state, it looked as though the British might win the war. The British had captured the colonists' supplies and taken many men prisoner. The British troops could roam the countryside freely, with little American resistance. The Continental Army had given Martha Bratton and her husband the responsibility to hold a supply of gunpowder on their property. Gunpowder was hard to find at this time. When Martha's husband was away, the British found out about the supply. They planned to steal it.

Martha heard about the British plan and made plans of her own. From the gunpowder kegs in storage, she laid a trail of gunpowder leading into the woods. Then, she hid in the woods and waited for the British to arrive. As the British troops approached, Martha put a match to the gunpowder trail. Soon, there was a great explosion and chaos among the troops. Martha was captured as she attempted to run away from the explosion. The British officer demanded to know who had set the gunpowder on fire. Martha proudly admitted that she had done it. Unexpectedly, the British let her go.

Sybil Ludington was another woman who took an active part in the war effort. Sybil's father was a colonel with a local American militia. Sybil and her parents were about to go to bed one evening. Suddenly, they heard the approach of a horse and then a pounding on the door. A young

Integrating American History with Reading Instruction © 2002 Creative Teaching Press

man who was very exhausted told them that the British had burned a nearby town and were coming this way. Someone needed to alert the militia. Colonel Ludington wanted to gather his men, but he also needed to be there when the British arrived. Before anyone could object, Sybil said she would warn the men. Off she rode on her horse.

This journey at night was a dangerous one. The road was not much more than a trail. At night, it was hard to see the obstacles that were in Sybil's path. In addition, the British could be anywhere, and she could be captured. However, Sybil rode as fast as she could through the night. She knocked on the doors of the militia members with a large stick. She told them to assemble at her father's house. Her warning allowed the militia to gather in time to drive the British back. Sybil Ludington is now known as the female Paul Revere.

When George Washington called for men to sign up for a professional full-time army, Deborah Sampson thought of a plan. She would enlist in his army. She cut her hair, tied a cloth around her chest, and put on men's clothes. She traveled far from home so no one would recognize her. She used her brother's name to enlist as a man in the Massachusetts regiment.

Deborah found the work and conditions more difficult than she had imagined. However, she worked hard for long hours and suffered through awful conditions. All this time, she also had to conceal her identity from the other soldiers. She did not mind because she was proud to be fighting for the American cause. Deborah was even wounded at one point. She was afraid the doctor would discover her true identity. Keeping quiet, she dug the bullet out of her thigh herself. Near the end of the war, Deborah became ill with a fever. She was so sick, she could hardly move or make a sound. The doctor discovered that his patient was a woman, not a frail young boy. He quietly treated her and never gave up her secret until after the war.

There are countless other women who were involved in the American cause for freedom. These women all chose to serve their country in a manner that was most important for them. Together, they helped America win its independence.

*Integrating American History with Reading Instruction © 2002 Creative Teaching Press*

# Comprehension Questions

## Literal Questions

1. What were the women of the American Revolution asked to do during the war?
2. Who concealed her identity to join the army?
3. What did Martha Bratton do to help in the American Revolution?
4. Who was known as the female Paul Revere?
5. Each of the women mentioned faced danger yet continued in her efforts. Describe at least one dangerous situation faced by each woman.

## Inferential Questions

1. Why do you think more women were not involved in the war efforts in direct ways such as the women described in the story?
2. What could have happened if the doctor had revealed Deborah Sampson's identity? Explain your answer.
3. How did these three women feel about sitting back and watching the war efforts? Explain your answer.
4. Compare and contrast the three women using a three-circle Venn diagram. List at least two ways they all are similar and two ways each woman is unique.
5. Sybil Ludington is now known as the female Paul Revere. Explain why this reference to Paul Revere makes sense.

## Making Connections

1. If you were asked to do further research on one of these women, which one would you want to learn more about? Why?
2. Describe three character traits you have that are similar to those the women in the story must have had. Explain why you think they are similar.
3. If you could travel back in time to ask any of these women one question, which woman would you choose? What would you ask? Why?
4. These women can be considered heroes. Have you known or heard of any people who have acted in a heroic way during your lifetime? If so, who was it and what did he or she do?
5. Do you think you would like to be part of the military when you grow up? If so, which branch (e.g., Army, Coast Guard, Navy, Marines) interests you the most? Why?

# Sharpen Your Skills

**1**  What is the best antonym for the word "approached" in the following sentence?

As the British troops **approached,** Martha Bratton put a match to the gunpowder trail.

- ⭕ withdrew
- ⭕ came up
- ⭕ entered
- ⭕ moved toward

**2**  How would you split the word "independence" into syllables?

- ⭕ in-depen-de-nce
- ⭕ i-ndep-en-dence
- ⭕ in-de-pen-dence
- ⭕ independen-dence

**3**  What part of speech is the word "in" in the following sentence?

Sybil Ludington was a woman who took an active part **in** the war effort.

- ⭕ preposition
- ⭕ interjection
- ⭕ adverb
- ⭕ conjunction

**4**  In which sentence is the word "drive" used in the same way as in the following sentence?

Her warning allowed the militia to gather in time to **drive** the British back.

- ⭕ Can I drive you to the store?
- ⭕ He is going to drive me crazy!
- ⭕ She helped drive the cattle back toward the water troughs.
- ⭕ Drive me to school, please.

**5**  Which words would finish this analogy?

**Gunpowder trail** is to _____ as **female Paul Revere** is to _____.

- ⭕ Bratton/Ludington
- ⭕ Bratton/Sampson
- ⭕ Sampson/Washington
- ⭕ Sampson/Ludington

**6**  What figure of speech does the following sentence include?

Deborah Sampson was as sly as a fox.

- ⭕ simile
- ⭕ exaggeration
- ⭕ metaphor
- ⭕ idiom

**7**  Which word best completes the following sentence?

The women _____ to be more involved than they were expected to be.

- ⭕ chosed
- ⭕ choosed
- ⭕ chosen
- ⭕ chose

*Integrating American History with Reading Instruction* © 2002 Creative Teaching Press

Name _____     Date _____

Room 17 is learning about women who played an active role in the American Revolution. The students are working in teams to make game boards. There are five teams. Each team has a different color and is making a game board for a different aspect of the role of women in the American Revolution. Use the clues below to decide the topic of each team's game board.

## Clues

**1** Neither the orange nor the yellow team made a game board featuring one particular woman of the era.

**2** The red team did not make a game board about the woman who impersonated a man in the army.

**3** The team that made a game board about the female Paul Revere was not blue or green.

**4** The team whose game board included clues about a woman who made a trail of gunpowder was not blue.

**5** The orange team focused their clues on the present times.

| | Red | Orange | Yellow | Green | Blue |
|---|---|---|---|---|---|
| Women's Roles in the Past | | | | | |
| Deborah Sampson | | | | | |
| Martha Bratton | | | | | |
| Sybil Ludington | | | | | |
| Women's Roles in the Present | | | | | |

The red team's game board topic was _____.

The orange team's game board topic was _____.

The yellow team's game board topic was _____.

The green team's game board topic was _____.

The blue team's game board topic was _____.

Integrating American History with Reading Instruction © 2002 Creative Teaching Press

# Hot Seat

## Purpose

The purpose of this activity is to have students take on the personality of a historical figure they read about. This will help students assimilate the information they have learned as well as experience a deeper understanding of what these women and others experienced during wartime.

### MATERIALS

✔ Historical Figure Description reproducibles (pages 39–41)

## Implementation

During this activity, students will pretend that they are one of the historical figures from the Historical Figure Description reproducibles. Tell students that the student on the "hot seat" will respond to questions from the historical figure's point of view. Choose one student to act as one historical figure. Have that student sit in a chair (i.e., hot seat) at the front of the classroom. Give each student a copy of the description of the historical figure the student will act out. Read aloud with students the description of that person. Encourage the student in the hot seat to follow along and listen carefully to the description so that he or she can begin to envision being the character. Have students ask the student in the hot seat questions related to the historical figure. Invite the student in the hot seat to think like, act like, and answer the questions the way he or she thinks the historical figure would. Encourage the other students to ask questions from the reproducible and/or create their own. Then, invite another student to sit in the hot seat, and repeat the activity with the same historical figure or a different one. An option is to divide the class into groups of students. Have one student in each group sit in the hot seat while the other students in the group interview him or her.

My name is Martha Bratton. I wanted to fight because...

HOT SEAT

*Integrating American History with Reading Instruction* © 2002 Creative Teaching Press

# Historical Figure Description

## Martha Bratton

Martha Bratton chose to get right in the middle of the war action. She lived in South Carolina. In her state, it looked as though the British might win the war. The British had captured the colonists' supplies and taken many men prisoner. The British troops could roam the countryside freely, with little American resistance. The Continental Army had given Martha Bratton and her husband the responsibility to hold a supply of gunpowder on their property. Gunpowder was hard to find at this time. When Martha's husband was away, the British found out about the supply. They planned to steal it.

Martha heard about the British plan and made plans of her own. From the gunpowder kegs in storage, she laid a trail of gunpowder leading into the woods. Then, she hid in the woods and waited for the British to arrive. As the British troops approached, Martha put a match to the gunpowder trail. Soon, there was a great explosion and chaos among the troops. Martha was captured as she attempted to run away from the explosion. The British officer demanded to know who had set the gunpowder on fire. Martha proudly admitted that she had done it. Unexpectedly, the British let her go.

## Questions for Martha Bratton

❶ Were you scared when you were asked to hide the gunpowder on your property? Why or why not?

❷ How did you feel when the British found out that you were hiding the gunpowder?

❸ Why did you hide in the woods?

❹ What gave you the idea to make a trail of gunpowder and then light it?

❺ Why did you admit to the British that you set the gunpowder trail on fire? Weren't you scared that they would arrest or kill you?

❻ Why do you think the British let you go?

Integrating American History with Reading Instruction © 2002 Creative Teaching Press

# Historical Figure Description

## Sybil Ludington

Sybil Ludington was another woman who took an active part in the war effort. Sybil's father was a colonel with a local American militia. Sybil and her parents were about to go to bed one evening. Suddenly, they heard the approach of a horse and then a pounding on the door. A young man who was very exhausted told them that the British had burned a nearby town and were coming this way. Someone needed to alert the militia. Colonel Ludington wanted to gather his men, but he also needed to be there when the British arrived. Before anyone could object, Sybil said she would warn the men. Off she rode on her horse.

This journey at night was a dangerous one. The road was not much more than a trail. At night, it was hard to see the obstacles that were in Sybil's path. In addition, the British could be anywhere, and she could be captured. However, Sybil rode as fast as she could through the night. She knocked on the doors of the militia members with a large stick. She told them to assemble at her father's house. Her warning allowed the militia to gather in time to drive the British back. Sybil Ludington is now known as the female Paul Revere.

## Questions for Sybil Ludington

❶ Were you proud that your father was a colonel? Why or why not?

❷ Who did you think was at your door at first? Who did it turn out to be?

❸ Why did you decide to ride off on your horse in the middle of the night?

❹ Why do you think your father allowed you to go alone?

❺ Why was riding off alone in the middle of the night a dangerous decision for you to make?

❻ Why are you sometimes called the female Paul Revere?

*Integrating American History with Reading Instruction © 2002 Creative Teaching Press*

# Historical Figure Description

## Deborah Sampson

When George Washington called for men to sign up for a professional full-time army, Deborah Sampson thought of a plan. She would enlist in his army. She cut her hair, tied a cloth around her chest, and put on men's clothes. She traveled far from home so no one would recognize her. She used her brother's name to enlist as a man in the Massachusetts regiment.

Deborah found the work and conditions more difficult than she had imagined. However, she worked hard for long hours and suffered through awful conditions. All this time, she also had to conceal her identity from the other soldiers. She did not mind because she was proud to be fighting for the American cause. Deborah was even wounded at one point. She was afraid the doctor would discover her true identity. Keeping quiet, she dug the bullet out of her thigh herself. Near the end of the war, Deborah became ill with a fever. She was so sick, she could hardly move or make a sound. The doctor discovered that his patient was a woman, not a frail young boy. He quietly treated her and never gave up her secret until after the war.

## Questions for Deborah Sampson

**1** Why did you want to enlist in Washington's army?

**2** What gave you the idea of creating a disguise? Why was that necessary?

**3** Did you enjoy being in the army? Why or why not?

**4** How did it feel knowing that you were fighting for your country?

**5** Were you scared that someone would discover your secret when you were very sick? Why or why not?

**6** Why do you think the doctor never told on you?

# Catch a Clue

slavery

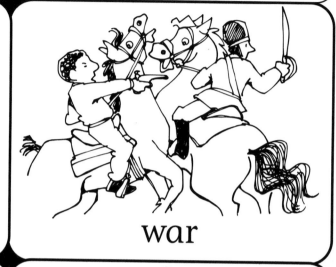

war

the right to vote

punishments for lawbreakers

**1** We will learn about some hardships many people had to endure.

**2** We will not learn about any historic battles.

**3** We will learn about the unfair treatment of men, women, and children who had not broken the law.

**4** We will learn about a courageous person who overcame being held against her will and later in life fought for equality of rights for all people.

# Concept Map

Facts we already know about **slavery,** and the new facts we have learned

**Slavery**

# Word Warm-Up

Which words might you expect to find in a story about **slavery?**

| | | |
|---|---|---|
| courageous | persuade | purchase |
| abolitionist | equality | furious |
| sheltered | labor | inspiration |
| citizens | dentist | transportation |

*Integrating American History with Reading Instruction* © 2002 Creative Teaching Press

# Sojourner Truth: Champion for Equality

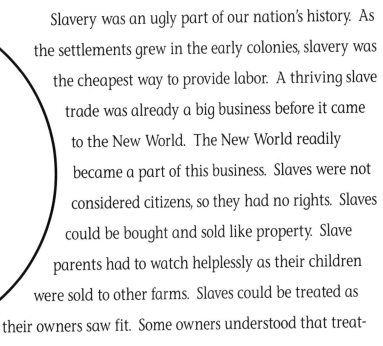

Slavery was an ugly part of our nation's history. As the settlements grew in the early colonies, slavery was the cheapest way to provide labor. A thriving slave trade was already a big business before it came to the New World. The New World readily became a part of this business. Slaves were not considered citizens, so they had no rights. Slaves could be bought and sold like property. Slave parents had to watch helplessly as their children were sold to other farms. Slaves could be treated as their owners saw fit. Some owners understood that treating slaves well could mean more labor from the slaves. However, many owners treated their slaves horribly. Slaves could be beaten, or even killed, without punishment to the owner. They lived in cabins with dirt floors, no windows, and cold drafts.

Sojourner Truth was born a slave sometime around 1797 in the state of New York. Her name then was Isabella. She had no last name. Sometimes historians refer to her as Isabella Baumfree because Baumfree was her father's first name. A Dutch family owned Isabella and her parents. Isabella learned to speak Dutch as a child. When she was young, she learned from her mother that she had older brothers and sisters. They had all been sold to other farms before Isabella had been born. She also learned about the love of God from her mother. Her mother told her to never give up hope of freedom. She said that God was always watching over Isabella.

Isabella was sold to another family nearby when she was eleven. This family spoke only English. Isabella could not understand what they asked her to do. Because of this, her owners thought she was lazy and ill-behaved. Her master bound her hands and beat her with a metal rod until her back was bloody. This was a horrible shock to Isabella. When she told her father about it, he was able to persuade a kinder man to purchase Isabella. This new owner treated Isabella well and she worked hard. She liked where she lived now, but still she thought about freedom. Isabella ended

Integrating American History with Reading Instruction © 2002 Creative Teaching Press

up with the Dumont family. The woman of the house married Isabella to another slave named Thomas. Together, Thomas and Isabella had five children.

In 1824, freedom became more possible for Isabella. New York had passed a law that would free all slaves who were at least twenty-eight years of age. Then, as other slaves reached that age, they would also be freed. Isabella did not know exactly when she had been born. Mr. Dumont told her that if she worked really hard, he would set her free in three years. When her Freedom Day came, the Dumonts would not set her free. Furious that they had gone back on their word, Isabella decided to escape. She was guided to the home of a Quaker family. They sheltered her and offered her protection. When Mr. Dumont found her anyway, the Quaker family purchased Isabella from him. In 1828, Isabella was finally set free.

In 1843, Isabella claimed that she received a command from God to preach. It was at this time that she chose her new name. "Sojourner" is a word from the Bible that means someone who moves from place to place. Sojourner would travel around the countryside preaching about God and freedom. When asked at one point what her last name was, she added Truth. She was preaching the truth as she knew it, and it would be a fitting name.

Sojourner Truth was a powerful speaker. Her voice was deep. She had deep faith and a quick wit. She traveled widely through New England and the Midwest, speaking about her beliefs. Sojourner met Frederick Douglass, an escaped slave who had taught himself to read and write. He now spoke out about the evils of slavery. She met William Lloyd Garrison, a well-known abolitionist. He wrote about the anti-slavery cause. These people had a big effect on Sojourner. She also began to speak out against slavery. In 1864, Sojourner met President Abraham Lincoln. She stayed in Washington, D.C., and worked to improve the living conditions for free blacks there. She helped find homes and jobs for escaped slaves. Sojourner spent the Civil War years in Battle Creek, Michigan. She continued to fight for the civil rights of slaves and for the equality of women until her death in 1883.

*Integrating American History with Reading Instruction © 2002 Creative Teaching Press*

# Comprehension Questions

## Literal Questions

1. What was Sojourner Truth's name at birth? How did she acquire her last name?
2. What is the meaning behind the name Sojourner Truth?
3. Where was she born? What approximate year is it thought she was born?
4. What year was Sojourner Truth given her freedom?
5. What circumstances led to her being freed from slavery?

## Inferential Questions

1. Why do you think people were allowed to treat slaves so poorly? How do you think Sojourner felt about this? Who else agreed with her point of view?
2. Sojourner's life changed dramatically many times. Create a time line to show the changes in her life. Record what you see to be the good times in one color and the bad times in another color.
3. How do you think she felt when she met Frederick Douglass and William Lloyd Garrison? Why?
4. Why do you think the title of the story is "Sojourner Truth: Champion for Equality"?
5. If Sojourner Truth could have looked into the future to see that slavery would have ended for all people in her near future, do you think she would have stopped preaching? Why or why not?

## Making Connections

1. How do you feel about slavery being part of our history?
2. Compare and contrast your life today with the lives of people who were slaves.
3. Describe three character traits you have that are similar to those of Sojourner Truth.
4. Sojourner Truth experienced a very tough situation. Many people might have given up on life after going through such a tough time, but she persevered. She worked for good causes. Was there a time in your life that you found challenging? What was it? How did you deal with it? In what ways did it make you a stronger person?
5. Sojourner helped out with many causes (e.g., anti-slavery, equality of women). What cause could you help with in your neighborhood or community?

# Sharpen Your Skills

**1** What is the best synonym for the word "persuade" in the following sentence?

Her father was able to **persuade** a kinder man to purchase Isabella.

- ○ hinder
- ○ decide
- ○ convince
- ○ argue

**2** Which of the following sentences does <u>not</u> end with the correct punctuation?

- ○ Sojourner Truth was finally set free in 1828?
- ○ Do you support her point of view?
- ○ She was born a slave and grew up to preach against slavery.
- ○ Sojourner Truth met many other anti-slave proponents.

**3** Which word is <u>not</u> a synonym for the word "furious" in the following sentence?

**Furious** that they had gone back on their word, Isabella decided to escape.

- ○ angry
- ○ excited
- ○ enraged
- ○ livid

**4** In which sentence is the word "free" used in the same way as in the following sentence?

In 1828, Isabella was finally set **free.**

- ○ I had a pass so the movie was free.
- ○ The fishermen set free some of the fish they caught.
- ○ The road was free of cars so I could cross the street safely.
- ○ I love when I get a free soda with my hamburger!

**5** Which words would finish this analogy?

**1843** is when Sojourner _____ as **1864** is when Sojourner _____.

- ○ died/changed her name
- ○ was born/became free
- ○ changed her name/became free
- ○ changed her name/met President Lincoln

**6** How would you split the word "equality" into syllables?

- ○ e-qua-li-ty
- ○ equal-ity
- ○ equ-al-i-ty
- ○ e-qu-al-ity

**7** Slaves were often mistreated even if they had not misbehaved.

What does the prefix "mis" mean?

- ○ before
- ○ bad; wrong
- ○ self
- ○ young

*Integrating American History with Reading Instruction © 2002 Creative Teaching Press*

# Get Logical

Five students are researching and reporting on one aspect of Sojourner Truth's life. Use the clues below to decide which aspect of her life each student reported on.

## Clues

**1** Neither Alice nor Laura reported on Sojourner's early childhood.

**2** Alice's report discussed equal rights for all people.

**3** Laura did not report on the toughest part of Sojourner's life.

**4** The inspiration Sojourner left behind for the next generation is highlighted in Dana's report.

**5** One aspect of James's report discussed Isabella learning to speak Dutch.

|  | Alice | Dana | Robert | James | Laura |
|---|---|---|---|---|---|
| Early Childhood |  |  |  |  |  |
| Horrible Years |  |  |  |  |  |
| Road to Freedom |  |  |  |  |  |
| Preaching Against Slavery |  |  |  |  |  |
| Legacy Left Behind |  |  |  |  |  |

Alice's report was on Sojourner's _____.

Dana's report was on Sojourner's _____.

Robert's report was on Sojourner's _____.

James's report was on Sojourner's _____.

Laura's report was on Sojourner's _____.

Integrating American History with Reading Instruction © 2002 Creative Teaching Press

# Fact or Fiction?

## Purpose

The purpose of this activity is to have students revisit and review facts they read about Sojourner Truth's life. This activity will also help students develop their skills in listening and following directions.

### MATERIALS

✔ Fact or Fiction? reproducibles (pages 51–52)

✔ index cards

✔ "Sojourner Truth: Champion for Equality" story (pages 45–46)

Sojourner Truth was born a slave.

Fact

Fact

## Implementation

Have students reread the story. Give each student two index cards. Ask students to write *Fact* on one card and *Fiction* on the second card. Read aloud a statement about slavery and Sojourner Truth's life from the Fact or Fiction? reproducible. Tell students that they will need to listen carefully to the statement and decide whether they think it is fact or fiction. Remind students that the entire statement must be true for it to be a fact. Then, have students raise one of their index cards to indicate their answer. After this kinesthetic part of the activity, give each student a Fact or Fiction? reproducible. Ask students to fill in the bubble that represents their answer. As an extension, have students write statements about another unit of study, compile them onto one page, and repeat the activity.

### Answer Key

| | | |
|---|---|---|
| 1. Fact | 2. Fiction | 3. Fact |
| 4. Fiction | 5. Fiction | 6. Fact |
| 7. Fact | 8. Fact | 9. Fiction |
| 10. Fact | 11. Fiction | 12. Fact |
| 13. Fiction | 14. Fiction | 15. Fact |
| 16. Fiction | 17. Fiction | 18. Fact |
| 19. Fact | 20. Fact | 21. Fiction |
| 22. Fact | 23. Fact | 24. Fiction |
| 25. Fact | 26. Fiction | 27. Fact |
| 28. Fact | 29. Fact | 30. Fact |

# Fact or Fiction?

**Directions:** Read each statement, and decide whether it is fact or fiction. Fill in the bubble that represents the correct answer.

**1** Sojourner Truth was born a slave.
  ○ Fact   ○ Fiction

**2** Our nation is proud of its heritage and its role in the slave trade.
  ○ Fact   ○ Fiction

**3** Slaves were bought and sold to work on plantations.
  ○ Fact   ○ Fiction

**4** Sojourner Truth enjoyed school and had a few friends.
  ○ Fact   ○ Fiction

**5** Sojourner Truth was born in Maryland.
  ○ Fact   ○ Fiction

**6** When Sojourner Truth was born, she had no last name.
  ○ Fact   ○ Fiction

**7** Some slaves were beaten, punished, and even killed.
  ○ Fact   ○ Fiction

**8** When Sojourner was given a last name, it was her father's first name.
  ○ Fact   ○ Fiction

**9** As a child, she lived with her brothers and sisters.
  ○ Fact   ○ Fiction

**10** She learned her perseverance from her mother.
  ○ Fact   ○ Fiction

**11** She lived with her family until she was 28 years old.
  ○ Fact   ○ Fiction

**12** She was misunderstood by some of her owners who thought she was lazy.
  ○ Fact   ○ Fiction

**13** Sojourner was never beaten by any of her owners.
  ○ Fact   ○ Fiction

**14** The Dumont family was the only family that owned Sojourner.
  ○ Fact   ○ Fiction

Integrating American History with Reading Instruction © 2002 Creative Teaching Press

# Fact or Fiction?

**15** She worked for a woman who married her to another slave.
○ Fact   ○ Fiction

**16** Sojourner and Thomas (her husband) had 15 children together.
○ Fact   ○ Fiction

**17** Sojourner gave up on ever becoming free. She knew she would remain a slave forever.
○ Fact   ○ Fiction

**18** In 1824, Mr. Dumont told Sojourner that if she worked really hard he would set her free in three years.
○ Fact   ○ Fiction

**19** The Dumont family lied. They did not set her free as they promised..
○ Fact   ○ Fiction

**20** She escaped and ended up with the Quaker family.
○ Fact   ○ Fiction

**21** The Dumonts discovered Sojourner at the Quaker family's home. They forced her to return with them.
○ Fact   ○ Fiction

**22** She was finally set free in 1828.
○ Fact   ○ Fiction

**23** She decided to become a preacher in 1843.
○ Fact   ○ Fiction

**24** She gave herself a new name in honor of her first sister who was still a slave.
○ Fact   ○ Fiction

**25** She began to speak out against slavery with Frederick Douglass and William Lloyd Garrison.
○ Fact   ○ Fiction

**26** She met President John Adams in 1864.
○ Fact   ○ Fiction

**27** She tried to make life better for some of the freed slaves by finding them jobs and homes.
○ Fact   ○ Fiction

**28** She fought for slaves to have civil rights.
○ Fact   ○ Fiction

**29** She fought for equality until she died in 1883.
○ Fact   ○ Fiction

**30** She is remembered today as a brave, strong-willed former slave who wanted freedom and justice for all.
○ Fact   ○ Fiction

*Integrating American History with Reading Instruction © 2002 Creative Teaching Press*

# Catch a Clue

## What will we learn about in our reading today?

Civil War

American Revolution

Lee    Sherman    Grant

military leaders

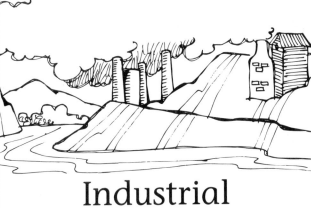

Industrial Revolution

**1** We will learn more about an important historical period.

**2** We will not learn about a time where there were protests because of imposed taxation.

**3** We will not be learning about a battle between the North and the South.

**4** We will learn about new innovations and the resulting changes that happened in the workplace.

# Concept Map

Facts we already know about the **Industrial Revolution,** and the new facts we have learned

*Integrating American History with Reading Instruction* © 2002 Creative Teaching Press

# Word Warm-Up

Which words might you expect to find in a story about the **Industrial Revolution?**

| | | |
|---|---|---|
| manufactured | harnessed | condenses |
| mine shafts | hoisted | locomotives |
| steam | freedom | techniques |
| chamber | children | misjudged |

# Industrial Revolution

Look all around. Many things are manufactured somewhere by a business. A group of businesses that manufacture the same type of product or provide similar services is called an industry. Clothes are made by businesses in the textile industry. A bus carries children to school. The bus and other vehicles are made by the transportation industry. A teenager has his teeth cleaned at the dentist. The dentist is a part of the health care industry.

There was a time years ago when broad changes were made in almost every industry. New techniques for producing goods and services developed. These changes happened rapidly. One invention led to another invention. The inventions dramatically affected the lives of people then and still do now. That is why it was called the Age of the Industrial Revolution.

The Industrial Revolution needed lots of power. At the beginning of the Industrial Age, animals provided that power. Mill wheels were powered by running water as well. Then, a new kind of power emerged: steam. By the end of the 18th century, the power of steam was being harnessed to replace the work of animals. Scientists knew that when water is heated, it expands and turns into steam. This causes pressure. When the steam cools, it condenses back into water. If steam is placed into an airtight container and cooled, the condensing steam will create a vacuum. This vacuum could be used to pull a piston. This was a good idea, but it took a long time before the iron industry could produce an airtight container.

Thomas Savery invented a working steam pump in 1698. It had no moving parts and was used to remove water from mine shafts. It was a good invention, but it was slow and used too much fuel to make steam. Then, Thomas Newcomen invented a better steam pump in 1712. This pump had moving parts and used less fuel to run. It was much safer than Savery's pump, too. Before long,

*Integrating American History with Reading Instruction © 2002 Creative Teaching Press*

Newcomen's pump engine was used all over England and Europe. In 1763, a man named James Watt was asked to repair a Newcomen pump engine. As he looked at the design, he realized that it was wasteful to keep heating and cooling the same chamber that held the steam. He added a separate chamber called a condenser. This condenser is where the steam would cool down. The main chamber would always stay hot, and therefore it used less fuel. Watt's new engine design was finished in 1769. Watt continued to improve upon his engine design. Each improvement made the engine more and more efficient.

As better engines were made, they were able to do more jobs. Engines hoisted coal and other minerals out of the mines. They ran spinning machines and weaving looms. Engines were used on farms to pull plows and separate grain from the husks. By the 1820s, the steam engine was used all over the world. At first, steam engines were too heavy to move. However, as the designs became smaller and more efficient, inventors experimented with the idea of a carriage that was powered by steam. The first attempts at a steam carriage were only slightly successful. Then, in 1804, an Englishman named Richard Trevithick built a steam engine that moved on iron tracks. He had managed to build a very lightweight engine that could move easily. The creation of this engine marked the beginning of the railroad industry. It led to the creation of locomotives and railroad lines. Now, people and goods could move quickly from place to place.

The greatest changes of the Industrial Revolution occurred within a period of 100 years. Machines began doing work that had always been done by hand. Machines could do this work faster and more efficiently. This was not always a good thing. Machines replaced workers and took away their jobs. People who had once been craftsmen were now working in factories. Often, these factories were dirty and dangerous. The work hours were long. There were no rules yet about children in the workplace, so very small children were sent to work in some factories. While the Industrial Revolution brought about new inventions and processes, it also brought about other problems that needed to be solved. Many of our labor laws and labor unions were a result of the conditions during the Industrial Revolution. The inventions of the Industrial Age changed our way of life forever and affect the way we do things to this day.

# Comprehension Questions

## Literal Questions

1. What did Thomas Savery invent? What year did he invent it?

2. Who invented a better steam pump in 1712? How was his invention an improvement?

3. What did Richard Trevithick invent? What year did he invent it? How was his invention helpful?

4. What difficulties did these inventions bring about?

5. The greatest changes of the Industrial Revolution occurred within a period of how many years?

## Inferential Questions

1. Why do you think some states do not allow people to have jobs until they are sixteen years old? Do you agree with this policy? Why or why not?

2. How do you think our current problems of global warming and the greenhouse effect might relate to the Industrial Revolution?

3. Most jobs only allow you to work eight hours. Beyond that, most employees earn extra money for the hours of overtime. Most full-time jobs provide health care benefits. Many jobs do not allow smoking inside the working environment. Compare and contrast current labor laws with the practices of the Industrial Revolution.

4. If you were to conduct an inspection of a factory back in the Industrial Revolution days, what problems might you find?

5. How do you think workers felt when their jobs were replaced by a machine? Why?

## Making Connections

1. In your opinion, did the Industrial Revolution make life better or worse for people? Write three reasons to support your opinion.

2. In what ways are the automobile industry and the health care industry alike? In what ways are they different?

3. Research the development of modern trains. Why were they important to the Industrial Revolution? What role did they play in trade and the economy?

4. What inventions have been created recently that affect your life today? Do they make life better or worse? Why?

5. Have you ever thought of an invention? Describe what it is, how you would build it, and how it works. How would it benefit other people?

*Integrating American History with Reading Instruction © 2002 Creative Teaching Press*

# Sharpen Your Skills

**1** Which word is an antonym for the word "broad" in the following sentence?

There was a time years ago when **broad** changes were made in almost every industry.

○ minimal          ○ large

○ widespread       ○ extensive

**2** Which of the following sentences uses the colon correctly?

○ James Watt's new engine design was finished: in 1769.

○ Then, a new kind of power emerged: steam.

○ Prior to the Industrial Age: animals provided most of the power.

○ Richard Trevithick's steam engine: was the beginning of the railroad industry.

**3** What part of speech is the word "dramatically" in the following sentence?

They **dramatically** affected the lives of people then and still do now.

○ preposition      ○ adverb

○ adjective        ○ conjunction

**4** What figure of speech does this sentence include?

She can run faster than a speeding train!

○ simile           ○ metaphor

○ irony            ○ idiom

**5** Which words would finish this analogy?

**Thomas Savery** is to _____ as **James Watt** is to _____.

○ steam pump/condenser   ○ locomotive/steam engine

○ condenser/steam pump   ○ steam engine/locomotive

**6** What does the word "It" refer to in the following sentences?

The creation of this engine marked the beginning of the railroad industry. **It** led to the creation of locomotives and railroad lines.

○ the beginning    ○ the railroad industry

○ the engine       ○ the creation

**7** Many of the practices that took place in the factories, including child labor, are now **illegal.** What does the prefix "il" mean in the word "illegal"?

○ not              ○ again

○ under            ○ before

Integrating American History with Reading Instruction © 2002 Creative Teaching Press

Name _____ Date _____

The Chief Executive Officers (CEOs) of five major corporations have personalized license plates. They are all grateful to have good labor laws for their employees as a result of the Industrial Revolution, so they display their thoughts in the message of their license plates. Use the clues below to decide which CEO has each personalized plate.

## Clues

❶ The shoe store CEO does not have the CONDNSE or the WEAREM plates.
❷ The CEO with the license plate in honor of James Watt does not work for a book publisher, a fast food chain, or a clothing company.
❸ The CEO who has the plates that honor Richard Trevithick does not work for the bank or book publisher.
❹ The CEO with the WEAREM plate likes to wear of lot of what he sells.
❺ The CEO for the fast food company does not have IM2BUSY or LOCOMTV.

|  | CEO of a bank | CEO of a clothing company | CEO of a shoe store | CEO of a fast food chain | CEO of a book publisher |
|---|---|---|---|---|---|
| WRKFAST |  |  |  |  |  |
| LOCOMTV |  |  |  |  |  |
| CONDNSE |  |  |  |  |  |
| WEAREM |  |  |  |  |  |
| IM2BUSY |  |  |  |  |  |

The WRKFAST plate belongs to the _____.

The LOCOMTV plate belongs to the _____.

The CONDNSE plate belongs to the _____.

The WEAREM plate belongs to the _____.

The IM2BUSY plate belongs to the _____.

*Integrating American History with Reading Instruction* © 2002 Creative Teaching Press

# Industrial Revolution Jeopardy

## Purpose

The purpose of this activity is for students to synthesize the information from the story they read about the Industrial Revolution in a game format. This game is based on the classic television game show called Jeopardy.

Integrating American History with Reading Instruction © 2002 Creative Teaching Press

### MATERIALS

✔ Jeopardy Questions (page 62)
✔ overhead transparency/ projector
✔ sticky notes

Who invented a working steam pump?

Thomas Savery!

## Implementation

Copy the Jeopardy Questions on an overhead transparency. Cover each box with a piece of a sticky-backed paper so it can be easily removed. Divide the class into groups of four to five students. Invite students to create a name for their team. Explain to students that they will play a game similar to Jeopardy, except they do not need to answer in the form of a question. Display the transparency. Pick a group to have the first turn. Tell students they have 10 seconds to decide on a category and point value. Read aloud the corresponding question. Tell students they have 30 seconds to discuss and agree on an answer and to pick one group member as a team speaker to answer. Ask students not to yell out the answer. If the answer is correct, they earn the point value of that question. If the answer is incorrect, allow another team's speaker to raise his or her hand to answer the question. Record the points on the chalkboard for the team that answers correctly.

### Answer Key

**Names:** 100—Industrial Revolution; 200—Thomas Savery; 300—James Watt; 400—Richard Trevithick; 500—Thomas Savery with the steam pump

**Facts:** 100—Health care industry; 200—Textile industry; 300—Animals; 400—To remove water from mine shafts/It was too slow and used too much fuel; 500—Hoisted coal and other minerals out of the mines; they ran spinning machines and weaving looms; were used on farms to pull plows and separate grain from husks

**Events:** 100—When water is heated, it expands and turns into steam. When water is cooled, it condenses back to water; 200—It used less fuel and was more efficient; 300—The invention of the lightweight engine; 400—It creates a vacuum; 500—Steam pump, condenser, and engine

**Dates:** 100—18th century; 200—1712; 300—1769; 400—1804; 500—100 year; approximately 1700–1800

# Jeopardy Questions

| | Names | Facts | Events | Dates |
|---|---|---|---|---|
| **100** | What is the name of the time period of rapid industrial growth? | What industry is a doctor part of? | What happens when water is heated? When it is cooled? | In which century did steam power begin to replace animal power? |
| **200** | Who invented the first working steam pump? | What industry is a clothing designer part of? | Why was the condenser a good invention? | When did Thomas Newcomen invent a better steam pump that led to pump engines being used throughout Europe? |
| **300** | Who added the condenser to Thomas Newcomen's pump engine? | What was the main power source before the Industrial Age? | What event led to the beginning of the railroad industry? | When did James Watt complete his new engine design? |
| **400** | Who created the first steam locomotive to move on iron tracks? | What was the first working steam pump used for? What were two problems with its design? | What will happen if steam is placed into an airtight container and cooled? | When was the first predecessor of the locomotive able to move on a track for the first time? |
| **500** | Who led us into the Industrial Revolution? How? | What role did steam engines play in the mining industry in the late 1700s? | What are three inventions that were important during the Industrial Revolution? | How long did the Industrial Revolution last? What do you estimate to be the beginning and end years? |

*Integrating American History with Reading Instruction © 2002 Creative Teaching Press*

# Catch a Clue

## What will we learn about in our reading today?

anti-slavery
protesters

George Washington    John Adams

first presidents
of the U.S.

Lee        Sherman        Grant

commanders of
the Civil War

early explorers
of America

**1** We will **not** focus on elected officials.

**2** We will discuss some individuals who led others through difficult times.

**3** We will **not** discuss people who paved the way for colonists and pioneers to make their way to the New World.

**4** We will focus on powerful decision-makers who were leaders during a divided time in history when sometimes brother fought against brother.

# Concept Map

Facts we already know about the **Civil War,** and the new facts we have learned

**Civil War**

*Integrating American History with Reading Instruction © 2002 Creative Teaching Press*

# Word Warm-Up

Which words might you expect to find in a story about the **Civil War?**

| | | |
|---|---|---|
| plagued | memoirs | lieutenant |
| secession | strategist | dignity |
| pneumonia | corruption | agricultural |
| personalities | amputated | graduate |

# Commanders of the Civil War

William T. Sherman

Ulysses S. Grant

Stonewall Jackson

The Civil War was a horrible chapter in the history of the United States. It was a war that pitted the North against the South. The Civil War took more American lives than any other war in history. It so divided the United States that in some families, brother fought against brother. The Southern states were trying to preserve slavery and an agricultural way of life. The Northern states supported a more modern way of life and an end to slavery. The fighting was bitter and bloody. The grief and bitterness was slow to go away. In some cases, it still exists. From this war, four great military personalities emerged. These men were Robert E. Lee, Ulysses S. Grant, William T. Sherman, and Stonewall Jackson.

Robert E. Lee was born in 1807. He came from a leading family in Virginia and served in the United States military. Lee greatly admired the accomplishments of George Washington and hated the thought of a divided union. However, he regarded the secession as the second war of independence. This time it was for the Confederacy. Lee was asked to command the Confederate army. This was a difficult decision for him because he was being asked to fight against the government he had always served. In the end, he decided to stay on the side of his home state, Virginia.

General Lee was known for his dignity and his calm, even in times of stress. He had a commanding appearance and was well respected by his men. He was never known to smoke, drink alcohol, or swear. General Lee was a brilliant strategist. His fame rests on his military achievements in spite of overwhelming odds. General Lee spent the last years of his life as the president of Washington College. General Robert E. Lee died in 1870.

Stonewall Jackson was born in 1824. He was religious by nature and careful about details. He believed in stern discipline and could get the maximum effort out of his troops. His soldiers loved and trusted him. Jackson was one of the best to fight under General Lee for the Confederacy. He

*Integrating American History with Reading Instruction* © 2002 Creative Teaching Press

received his nickname during the first battle of Bull Run. Against all odds, Jackson's troops formed a strong line and held its ground against the Union army. A colleague saw Jackson and commented that he stood there like a stone wall. The name stuck from then on: Stonewall Jackson. During the war, Jackson was accidentally shot by his own troops. Although his arm was amputated to save his life, he died of pneumonia eight days later in 1863. After Jackson's death, General Lee could find no one worthy of replacing him.

Ulysses S. Grant was born in 1822. Grant was a highly moral man. Always shy and reserved, he spoke only when he had something to say. Grant was not concerned with outward appearances. His one bad habit was smoking cigars, a habit that eventually killed him. Grant freed his only slave in 1859 and strongly opposed the secession. When the war broke out, he felt it was his duty to fight for the Union. President Lincoln was very disappointed in the Union leadership at the beginning of the war. After Grant had a series of military successes, Lincoln placed him at the head of the Union forces. He turned out to be a brilliant military commander. Grant was criticized for the heavy Union losses. However, his strong military leadership helped turn the war in favor of the North. Ulysses S. Grant was elected President in 1868. Unfortunately, he was not as successful here as he had been in the military. Corruption and problems plagued his administration. Just as he finished his memoirs, Grant died of cancer in 1885.

William T. Sherman was born in 1820. He became General Grant's most trusted lieutenant. Sherman could be nervous and irritable. He slept very little and talked a lot. He distrusted newspapermen and politicians. Sherman was given the task of leading Union troops to the city of Atlanta, Georgia. Sherman led an army that eventually took Atlanta and burned it to the ground. He hoped that the vast destruction would break the will of the South and end the war. Sherman's Union troops then continued their march through Georgia and the Carolinas.

These four men had always been a part of the United States military. The circumstances of the Civil War made it necessary for them to fight against each other.

Integrating American History with Reading Instruction © 2002 Creative Teaching Press

# Comprehension Questions

## Literal Questions

1. Who did Robert E. Lee admire? What was Lee's role in the Civil War?
2. Who was criticized for the heavy Union losses?
3. Who was accidentally shot by his own troops in the war? What caused his death?
4. Who was Stonewall Jackson? What was his role in the Civil War?
5. How did Stonewall Jackson get his nickname?

## Inferential Questions

1. Compare the backgrounds of all of the commanders. What did they have in common? How were they different?
2. Why couldn't General Lee find a replacement for Stonewall Jackson? Do you think that his death was related to the outcome of the Civil War in any way? Explain your thinking.
3. All of the men in the story were educated men. How do you think their education was relevant to the war?
4. Why do you think the commanders were chosen to become leaders?
5. How do you think history would have been altered if the Civil War had never taken place?

## Making Connections

1. If you had to fight in the Civil War, which of the men in the story would you want as your commanding officer? Why?
2. How has the army changed since the Civil War? Research the current enlistment procedures and living conditions. Compare them with those at the time of the Civil War.
3. If you worked for a major toy company and could recommend making only one of these commanders into an action figure, who do you think deserves the honor? Why?
4. Did any of your relatives fight in the Civil War? Talk with your family members to find out more about what that relative did during the Civil War.
5. The Emancipation Proclamation also cleared the way for African Americans to serve in the military. Research the history of African Americans in the military.

*Integrating American History with Reading Instruction © 2002 Creative Teaching Press*

# Sharpen Your Skills

**1** What is the best synonym for the word "stern" in the following sentence?

Stonewall Jackson believed in **stern** discipline and could get the maximum effort out of his troops.

- ○ relentless
- ○ light
- ○ strict
- ○ moderate

**2** Which of the following sentences does <u>not</u> have correct comma usage?

- ○ William T. Sherman the West Point graduate was General Grant's, most trusted lieutenant.
- ○ Yes, the Civil War resulted in numerous deaths.
- ○ The report on Ulysses S. Grant was, of course, fantastic.
- ○ General Robert E. Lee, the Civil War commander, died in 1870.

**3** What part of speech is the word "bloody" in the following sentence?

The fighting throughout the Civil War was bitter and **bloody.**

- ○ preposition
- ○ adjective
- ○ adverb
- ○ conjunction

**4** How would you split the word "achievements" into syllables?

- ○ achieve-ments
- ○ a-chieve-ments
- ○ ach-iev-ments
- ○ a-ch-iev-me-nts

**5** Which words would finish this analogy?

**Robert E. Lee** is to _____ as **Ulysses S. Grant** is to _____.

- ○ Confederate/Union
- ○ Union/Confederate
- ○ president/commander
- ○ William T. Sherman/Stonewall Jackson

**6** What figure of speech does this sentence include?

Some commanders were as tough as nails.

- ○ simile
- ○ exaggeration
- ○ metaphor
- ○ idiom

**7** What does the prefix "un" mean in the following sentences?

The Civil War was an unhappy time in American history. It was not uncommon for brother to fight against brother.

- ○ again
- ○ before
- ○ self
- ○ not

Integrating American History with Reading Instruction © 2002 Creative Teaching Press

Name _____   Date _____

Nolan, Sheila, Maddie, Jeff, and Jay are each writing a report on the Civil War. Four of the students are writing about the different commanders. The fifth student is writing about the outcomes of the war. Use the clues below to decide which topic each student is preparing a report on.

## Clues

**1** Sheila wrote her report on a lieutenant who led Union troops to the city of Atlanta, Georgia.
**2** Neither Jeff nor Nolan wrote about a commander who was shot by his own troops.
**3** Jay did not write a report on a single commander or officer.
**4** Nolan wrote a report about a commander who was known for his calmness even in times of stress.

|  | Nolan | Sheila | Maddie | Jeff | Jay |
|---|---|---|---|---|---|
| Robert E. Lee |  |  |  |  |  |
| Ulysses S. Grant |  |  |  |  |  |
| William T. Sherman |  |  |  |  |  |
| Stonewall Jackson |  |  |  |  |  |
| Outcomes of the War |  |  |  |  |  |

Nolan's report was on _____.

Sheila's report was on _____.

Maddie's report was on _____.

Jeff's report was on _____.

Jay's report was on _____.

*Integrating American History with Reading Instruction © 2002 Creative Teaching Press*

# Time Line of the Civil War

## Purpose

The purpose of this activity is to help students better understand the events prior to, during, and after the American Civil War. Students will research key events and the date each event occurred and then sequence the information on a time line.

### MATERIALS

- ✔ Civil War Events reproducible (page 72)
- ✔ research materials (e.g., Internet, books, encyclopedias)
- ✔ 12" x 18" (30.5 cm x 46 cm) construction paper
- ✔ scissors
- ✔ tape
- ✔ rulers
- ✔ crayons or markers

## Implementation

Give each student a Civil War Events reproducible. Provide research materials, and have students work in groups or individually to research each event listed on the reproducible and record the date it took place. Review the answers as a whole class, and invite students to change any incorrect answers. Then, give each student a piece of construction paper. Tell students to fold their paper in half like a hot dog and then cut along the crease. Ask them to tape together the two short edges of the paper. Have students place their paper horizontally in front of them. Tell students to use a ruler to measure 3 inches (7.5 cm) down from the top and draw a line across the middle of the entire paper. Invite them to measure and mark off every 5 inches (12.5 cm) on the line with a small mark that will represent a year. Ask students to label their time line with the years 1861–1865. Encourage them to use the information from their completed reproducible to write each date and event across their time line. Invite students to illustrate and color some of the events as well.

### Answer Key

1.  April 26, 1865
2.  November 23–25, 1863
3.  November 8, 1864
4.  January 1, 1863
5.  April 12, 1861
6.  April 6–7, 1862
7.  April 19, 1861
8.  May 26, 1865
9.  May 11, 1865
10. February 6, 1862
11. April 15, 1861
12. February 16, 1862
13. April 14, 1865
14. April 16, 1862
15. July 1–3, 1863
16. March 9, 1864
17. September 22, 1862
18. May 21, 1861
19. February 6, 1865
20. August 27–30, 1862
21. April 9, 1865
22. April 2, 1865
23. July 21, 1861

Name _____     Date _____

# Civil War Events

**Directions:** Research each event and write the date it took place. Use the information at the bottom of the page as a reference.

**1** Johnston surrendered to Sherman on _____.

**2** The Battle of Chattanooga happened on _____.

**3** Abraham Lincoln was reelected as President on _____.

**4** President Lincoln issued the Emancipation Proclamation on _____.

**5** Confederate troops attacked Fort Sumter on _____.

**6** The Battle at Shiloh was won by the Union on _____.

**7** Lincoln blocked off the South on _____.

**8** The last of the Confederate troops surrendered on _____.

**9** Jefferson Davis was captured on _____.

**10** Union forces took Fort Henry on _____.

**11** President Lincoln issued a call for the troops on _____.

**12** Grant's troops took Fort Donelson on _____.

**13** President Lincoln was assassinated on _____.

**14** Soldiers began to be drafted for the Confederacy on _____.

**15** The North won the Battle of Gettysburg on _____, which marked a turning point in the Civil War.

**16** Grant became General in Chief for the North on _____.

**17** President Lincoln issued a preliminary Emancipation Proclamation on _____.

**18** Richmond, Virginia, became the Confederate capital on _____.

**19** Lee became General in Chief for the South on _____.

**20** The Second Battle of Bull Run, where the South won, happened on _____.

**21** Lee surrendered at Appomattox on _____.

**22** The cities of Petersburg and Richmond were given up by Confederate troops on _____.

**23** The Battle of Bull Run ended as the Northern troops left on _____.

| April 12, 1861 | April 15, 1861 | April 19, 1861 | May 21, 1861 |
| --- | --- | --- | --- |
| July 21, 1861 | February 6, 1862 | February 16, 1862 | April 6–7, 1862 |
| April 16, 1862 | August 27–30, 1862 | September 22, 1862 | January 1, 1863 |
| July 1–3, 1863 | March 9, 1864 | November 23–25, 1863 | November 8, 1864 |
| February 6, 1865 | April 2, 1865 | April 9, 1865 | April 14, 1865 |
| April 26, 1865 | May 11, 1865 | May 26, 1865 | |

*Integrating American History with Reading Instruction © 2002 Creative Teaching Press*